Creating a Sustainable Brand

A Guide to Growing the Sustainability Top Line

Henk Campher
Senior Vice President, Business + Social Purpose & Managing Director,
Sustainability at Edelman
Email: **henk.campher@edelman.com**

First published in 2014 by Dō Sustainability

87 Lonsdale Road, Oxford OX2 7ET, UK

ISBN 978-1-910174-07-4 (eBook-ePub)

ISBN 978-1-910174-08-1 (eBook-PDF)

ISBN 978-1-910174-06-7 (Paperback)

A catalogue record for this title is available from the British Library.

Dō Sustainability strives for net positive social and environmental impact. See our sustainability policy at **www.dosustainability.com**.

Page design and typesetting by Alison Rayner

Cover by Becky Chilcott

For further information on Dō Sustainability, visit our website: **www.dosustainability.com**

DōShorts

Dō Sustainability is the publisher of **DōShorts**: short, high-value ebooks that distil sustainability best practice and business insights for busy, results-driven professionals. Each DōShort can be read in 90 minutes.

New and forthcoming DōShorts – stay up to date

We publish 3 to 5 new DōShorts each month. The best way to keep up to date? Sign up to our short, monthly newsletter. Go to **www. dosustainability.com/newsletter** to sign up to the Dō Newsletter. Some of our latest and forthcoming titles include:

- *Strategic Sustainability: Why it Matters to Your Business and How to Make it Happen*   Alexandra McKay
- *Sustainability Decoded: How to Unlock Profit Through the Value Chain*   Laura Musikanski
- *Working Collaboratively: A Practical Guide to Achieving More* Penny Walker
- *Understanding G4: The Concise Guide to Next Generation Sustainability Reporting*   Elaine Cohen
- *Leading Sustainable Innovation*   Nick Coad & Paul Pritchard
- *Leadership for Sustainability and Change*   Cynthia Scott & Tammy Esteves
- *The Social Licence to Operate: Your Management Framework for Complex Times*   Leeora Black
- *Building a Sustainable Supply Chain*   Gareth Kane
- *Management Systems for Sustainability: How to Successfully Connect Strategy and Action*   Phil Cumming

- *Understanding Integrated Reporting: The Concise Guide to Integrated Thinking and the Future of Corporate Reporting* Carol Adams
- *Corporate Sustainability in India: A Practical Guide for Multinationals* Caroline Twigg
- *Networks for Sustainability: Harnessing People Power to Deliver Your Goals* Sarah Holloway
- *Making Sustainability Matter: How To Make Materiality Drive Profit, Stragegy and Communications* Dwayne Baraka

Subscriptions

In addition to individual sales of our ebooks, we now offer subscriptions. Access 60+ ebooks for the price of 5 with a personal subscription to our full e-library. Institutional subscriptions are also available for your staff or students. Visit **www.dosustainability.com/books/subscriptions** or email **veruschka@dosustainability.com**

Write for us, or suggest a DōShort

Please visit **www.dosustainability.com** for our full publishing programme. If you don't find what you need, write for us! Or suggest a DōShort on our website. We look forward to hearing from you.

....

Abstract

THE CHANGES EXPERIENCED IN SUSTAINABILITY over the last ten years or so have been nothing but phenomenal. More and more companies have embraced the need to act more responsibly and manage their impacts. What started as 'doing less harm' has turned into bottom line benefits as companies have found new ways to match managing the triple bottom line with shaving costs off the business bottom line. But you don't cut yourself into growth and growth is the bread and butter of companies. And it's the holy grail of sustainability – growing the business top line. That's why we need consumers to come and join the party – they already do, just look at TOMS, Patagonia, Method, Seventh Generation, Dove and many more. What is missing isn't the consumer but a better grip on what makes them tick – a sustainable brand they can trust, buy and advocate. This book cuts through the myths and noise to create a sustainable brand model, a fusion of product and branding. It's when these two dance that we create consumer breakthrough and the magic happens. But let's not get ahead of ourselves. Let's simply create more sustainable brands – and this is the 'how to' guide that will help you get there.

About the Author

CHALLENGE CONVENTIONAL THINKING and have fun – with 20 years of global experience, **Henk Campher** is known as a disruptive and creative expert in the sustainability space. He's had the pleasure of working on some of the coolest campaigns with companies such Starbucks, Levi's, Best Buy, Timberland, Tiffany's and Nestlé. He has been bridging the world of nerds (sustainability experts) and flirts (communication whizzes) thanks to being part of team Edelman in the USA, his time in the UK as an Oxfam campaigner, and his South African roots as an African development worker, trade unionist and creator of the Nelson Mandela initiated Proudly South African campaign. He was named as one of the Top 100 Thought Leaders in Trustworthy Business Behavior and *The Guardian*'s Top 15 Sustainable Business Executives on Twitter. Henk is a regular blogger at Triple Pundit and CSRWire, a frequent speaker at conferences, and a Twitter junkie: **@AngryAfrican**.

Acknowledgments

TO THE THREE MOST IMPORTANT PEOPLE IN MY LIFE, Heidi, Emma and Lili, thank you for your patience and encouragement. You are my inspiration and the reason I wrote this book. And to Sir Biscuit and the cats.

To my friends who never knew they were also my mentors – especially Heather, Scott, Todd, Lisa, Paul, Michele, Sue, Manny, Ghilly, Jakes, Suzie, Nicola, Herman, Mark, Rafael, Leah, Lizard-lips and Delboy. What a privilege to be your friend.

To my awesome Edelman family who are all the right mix of funny and fearless. Too many to mention but a special shout-out to Carol, Christine, Veronica, Rebecca, Peter, Adrienne, Dolleen, Katie, Jaci, Jackie, Morgan, Lisa, Jeremy, Alex, Ashley, Beata, Josh, Larry and all the Business + Social Purpose geniuses.

And to Richard, Matt, Alan, Mark, Ben, Julianna, KB, Ravi, Harlan and Maria – thank you for pushing us never to be happy with average, for willing us on to be disruptive and to be ourselves, and for always believing in us. It's an honor to be part of team Edelman.

A special thanks to Elise and Sam for the editing and helping me fix the many mistakes and making it so much better. I promise never to do that again.

To Nick Bellorini from Dō Sustainability for reviewing and publishing this book. And for being extremely patient. . . And to Gudrun Freese for the brainstorming and marketing help.

ACKNOWLEDGMENTS

A special thanks to the brand whizzes, sustainability junkies, Twitter hacks, opinion bloggers, media wonks, lovely and complex clients, and to the Joel's, Marc's, Aman's, David's, Leon's and Nick's of the world – you are my teachers and gurus. Thank you for that and for all the chats and challenges that made this book possible.

To the many missed names of mentors, friends, clients and colleagues of today and yesterday – you made me a better person and I am sorry that I forgot to put your name in here. Next drink is on me.

To the businesses I admire, the leaders I look up to, the activists who motivate me, and the people I meet in the streets who move me to action – I won't mention you because it won't be fair, but never stop being you. You make the difference.

Finally, a special thanks to the heroes who inspire me – Nelson Mandela, Desmond Tutu, Anita Roddick, Robert Davies and the people back home in Africa who taught me Ubuntu. I hope I make you proud.

Contents

CONTENTS

PART 1

The Changing World of a Sustainable Brand

1. The search for a sustainable brand

FOR MOST COMPANIES the holy grail of sustainability is a breakthrough with consumers. We live in a world where competing on price and quality alone has become increasingly difficult. Consumers expect more from brands but companies remain mostly disillusioned with the lack of consumer support for sustainability. On the other hand, consumers don't trust businesses and are weary of greenwashing and empty promises. Somewhere there is a disconnect between what consumers want and what companies are offering them. How do we bridge this gap? The answer lies in knowing what a sustainable brand is and how a company can or cannot create a sustainable brand relevant to their product and brand promise. The aim of this book is to define what a sustainable brand is and to provide a model to guide the development of a sustainable brand. But let's start at the beginning – the changing world of sustainability.

2. The changing world of sustainability

We've gone a long way down this sustainability road. We've found new and innovative ways to cut the impact(s) that companies have on the environment and society by switching off lights, turning off taps and recycling waste. We've even found new ways to measure all of these good things we've done through our commitments to cut carbon, report to the latest GRI G4 levels and fine-tuning materiality assessments in order to focus on those areas where we have the greatest impacts. Heck, we've even had time to create a few new concepts like shared value and carbon neutrality.

Those lauded as being at the leading edge of sustainability have managed to tie their sustainability initiatives to business benefits. It's not just about cutting carbon but reducing energy use to reduce that energy bill. It's not just about recycling but finding new ways to reuse and repurpose to help the business bottom line. We didn't just turn off the taps; we managed to save money by recycling water. Every good act had a societal benefit and a positive business impact on the business bottom line.

But has all this 'doing less bad' helped us get closer to creating a sustainable world? We've focused so much attention on doing less harm in the hope that it will create a more sustainable world that we've forgotten to focus on the most important part of business – the top line. Reducing costs through efficiencies is great but successful businesses are judged on growth. You don't grow a business by cutting cost or spark growth by only looking at the business bottom line. Could it be that, despite all the cost savings and business bottom line focus, we've yet to bring sustainability to the heart of business?

Maybe the answer lies in bringing sustainability to those who bring growth to companies. Those pesky things called consumers.

3. The pesky consumer

Assumption 1: The consumer

This book uses the term *consumer* to describe a person or organization that uses a product or service. This definition therefore includes Business-to-Consumer and Business-to-Business relationships and refers to what some businesses might call customers, shoppers, buyers, users, purchasers or even punters.

As often as they conduct materiality assessments and engage with all stakeholders to define the areas where the greatest impacts are, companies care about two groups of people – those who can take their money away and those who can give them money. There are very few groups who can take their money away: competitors can via a new product that consumers prefer or by finding a new value proposition that resonates with consumers. Regulators can through taxes, fines and regulations. Activists hope they can but very few activist campaigns hurt the business bottom line of companies. But from a growth perspective, we want to focus on those who can help companies make money – the consumer. Yes, investors will invest and give money to companies but only insofar as they believe that the company will make money through growth. Investors don't stimulate growth; only increased consumption of the company's products or services creates growth. So what we really need to focus on is the consumer in order to bring sustainability to the business top line.

This is the holy grail of sustainability after all – getting more consumers to buy into the idea of sustainability. Or more specifically, getting more consumers to buy truly sustainable products – even if they do sometimes cost more. But it seems as if we will never really get there and this is validated by the experts and leaders in the sustainability field.

Marc Gunther, a leading light in the sustainability field, wrote about the *elusive green consumer*, pointing out that while market research shows that consumers want greener products, their purchasing behavior doesn't follow suit. Similarly, *Triple Pundit* has shared statistics about consumers (becoming) increasingly skeptical of green products (**http:// goo.gl/8IRuKO**). And we were told by GreenBiz that we need a dose of reality (**http://goo.gl/Zfwvnx**) when it comes to the presence (or absence) of green consumers. It's enough to drive us crazy – this elusive pesky green consumer. Or maybe we need to reassess the ways we look at consumers when we use our sustainability lens.

But let's start with the question of whether consumer behavior has changed when it comes to sustainability. Is it true to think that consumer behavior hasn't changed?

4. Changing consumer behavior

Of course it has. It has changed around us every single day – and continues to do so. But it is difficult to see it grow. Maybe it is because we desire rapid and immediate change – whether the MTV generation or the reality show generation, we all want our 'fix' right away. Quick fame and fast money. But consumer behavior is less revolution and more evolution. Like everything else in evolution it moves slowly but surely. But don't expect to see a big moment in time where it hits you in the face. You'll have more luck watching the grass grow or the paint dry. But over time, we have to recognize the changes.

Let's just consider how much the world has changed over the last 20 to 30 years.

- **Fairtrade:** Remember when Fair Trade (http://goo.gl/yxcMHx) was just a little sparkle in the eyes of activists? Today it continues to grow at a rapid pace, outstripping the growth of more 'traditional' ways of doing business – growing globally by 12 percent in 2011 alone (http://goo.gl/73uY2C).

- **Auto:** How are those hybrid sales going? Yes, they may still be behind traditional car sales but sales of electric and hybrid cars grew by 72 percent in 2012 and were the fastest growing sector in the US automotive industry (http://goo.gl/hMe3H).

- **Cleaning & personal products:** How about those Method guys? Or Seventh Generation? Or Greenworks? New cleaning products are coming onto the market almost daily. And how about Dove soap? It was 'just another bar of soap' until Unilever (http://goo.gl/Rt5UN4) adopted *real beauty for* women, a popular social issue, and turned that into a core brand quality and differentiator. It didn't just transform the brand but changed the whole product category. And it was done focusing on one of the three key pillars of sustainability – social issues – and how that intersects with both the brand and the target consumers.

- **Clothing:** TOMS has been a bit of a revelation, right? Patagonia continues to disrupt the marketplace through their edgy sustainability initiatives and positioning. Notice how clothing companies like Levi's and Timberland are constantly bringing new sustainable products to the consumer and adding new value to their business top line and values bottom line. Timberland Earthkeepers played a key part in transforming the business during a difficult time for the company. Even today Earthkeepers is Timberland's fastest growing and largest product line (**http://goo.gl/IU6GqU**).

- **Food:** Have you noticed changes in your milk lately and how it doesn't have as many hormones or other unsavory ingredients in it anymore? Have you noticed how organic products have grown far faster than most other consumer products? Walk through grocery stores today and you'll see the huge variety of green, ethical, organic goods on the shelf today. No one thinks of Stonyfield Farms as some hippie yogurt business anymore. Or Ben & Jerry's as some small ice cream company.

Imagine how few of those products were on that same shelf 20 years ago. Many of these products have become mainstream. They are so much a part of our lives today that we forget that they are still new when considering the life of a consumer product.

Sales continue to grow each year and new products create breakthroughs almost continuously. And consumers are buying them. Some are growing fast and some not so fast. That is simply the nature of the beast – it grows and will continue to grow.

Just don't expect a revolution. It's not – it's an evolution. Maybe part of the reason is because of a natural progression along the hierarchy of increasingly rich societies and better off people having different tastes, even if only marginally. Whatever the reasons, things happen but they usually happen slower than expected. Not every product is an iPhone – some take time to grow.

Not only do consumers buy more sustainable products each and every day but companies are using this evolution to transform their products and brands to drive new growth in sales and consumer support. We need to realize that sustainable products have grown up faster than we did – and so have consumers. We are wrong when we think consumers aren't buying into sustainability and aren't buying products and brands they believe add to a more sustainable lifestyle and world. They are but not the way we want it. And that is our problem, not theirs. This is a business problem to solve, not a consumer's. We know they want to buy sustainable products (or products with sustainability as part of the brand value proposition) and we know they want to buy more.

The biggest question isn't whether consumers are buying green or sustainable products. We know they are. And we know they want to buy more of these sustainable products. The problem is to find better ways to bring sustainability to life for the consumers in ways that will resonate with them, and foster even faster growth. To find the solution we need to look closer at brand – the soul of a product identity.

5. The need for brand transformation

Almost every consumer study shows the consistent changes in consumer behavior when it comes to sustainability. The SustainAbility, Globescan and BBMG study (**http://goo.gl/gwUksB**) shows that we now have more than 2 billion aspirational consumers that combine style, status and sustainability. That is over two thirds of the global consumer population. Even more important, that is almost half of the primary shoppers of each household. This fast-growing group stands out as they are more advanced in the sustainable consumption world than other shoppers

– they believe they need to consume less to preserve the environment for future generations (92%), compared to 75% of all consumers. But what make this group attractive to companies aren't their sustainability commitments. What makes them attractive is that they are the dream consumer for most companies.

TABLE 1. Aspirational consumers vs all consumers

Issue	Aspirational consumers	All consumers
Gets excited by shopping for new things	78%	48%
Trusts companies to do the right thing	58%	52%
Wants to stand out in look and style	73%	53%
Advocates and encourages others to buy from responsible companies	88%	63%
Willing to pay more for sustainable products	91%	64%

They are also from the most desired group of consumers – the younger and urban. Millennials make up 40% of this group, GenX 37% and 59% live in urban areas. Furthermore, they are in the key markets like China (46% of population), India (42%) and USA (36%).

These are the consumers companies are hoping to attract. Consumers who want style and sustainability. Consumers who will trust companies when they do the right thing. Consumers who will buy from companies doing the right thing. And consumers who will encourage others to do the same. Young, hip, urban and ready to buy. And they are here and ready, today.

CREATING A SUSTAINABLE BRAND:
A GUIDE TO GROWING THE SUSTAINABILITY TOP LINE

Edelman's brandshare study (**http://goo.gl/rtmHEh**) confirms this hypothesis that consumers overwhelmingly want to buy, use, recommend and support brands who share their values. It is the great unmet demand. In fact, 90% of people across the world want brands to share with them. Yes, the consumer is ready and they are ready to transform the world at a much faster pace than has happened so far. So why aren't they?

The challenge is that the same study shows that only 10% of consumers think that brands share their values. They do not believe that brands meet their demand for responsible products and services. This '80% opportunity gap' very simply shows that there is a disconnect between what consumers want and what they believe brands give them. This is further supported by the Edelman Trust Barometer study (**http://goo.gl/gKZ7HU**) that shows only 19% of people believe business is helping to solve societal or social issues. The challenge is therefore not that consumers don't care but rather that brands do not know how to bring sustainability to life for consumers. What is needed is not a change in behavior from the consumer side, but rather better ways for brands to bring sustainability to life in and through their brands. We need a change in behavior from brands.

This is the great unmet demand – brands bringing sustainability to life for consumers, embedding it into the brand and product in new and compelling ways for consumers to understand, support, advocate and buy.

Of course companies will fail if they try to sell products based primarily on their sustainability merits. No one buys a car to go from point A to point B – okay, maybe a small percentage of deeply ethically minded consumers will give up everything else to buy purely sustainable products. For most consumers, sustainability is only one element of the value proposition that the brand holds, just one of many reasons why they love and support a brand. They don't buy just because of cold hard facts. They buy the dream of wind blowing in their hair and driving the road less traveled – and then we wake up stuck in the two hour-long commute to work. People buy products and brands for many reasons – sometimes because of the price and sometimes because of the quality. And sometimes they love a product because of the dream that it sells. Or the memories it evokes. And sometimes the brand promises sexiness or seriousness or playfulness or many combinations of promises and emotions. There are many reasons why people love and buy products and brands. The same rules apply to brands that embed sustainability into their brand promise. They need to remain true to the brand and find authentic ways to embed sustainability into the brand. It needs to enhance the brand promise and the brand value proposition that resonates with the consumer. And it will be different for each brand. Each brand will have to find its own unique way of bringing to life the promise sustainability holds for the brand – and for the consumer. Sustainability then becomes one part of the value proposition just as price, quality, functionality, tone, personality, etc. are part of the value proposition and brand identity. Of course making sustainability part of this isn't easy but we have enough examples out there to start defining how this can be done.

Assumption 2: The brand

Brand in this book is not meant to be limited to a consumer and/or product brand. It can also be used to describe a corporate brand as most of the rules remain the same when building a brand with sustainability embedded in its value proposition. The consumer might be different but the brand is still 'consumed' by its customers – investors, regulators, etc.

PART 2

The Birth of a Brand

1. (Sustainable) brand development

Assumption 3: Product definition

The term *product* will be used throughout this book. However, the meaning of product in this book is simply that it is the object of the transaction between the company and the consumer. It is not limited to a physical object or commodity but can include services for hire or sale and products and services that are physical, virtual or found in cyberspace. The term *product* is used for flow and ease of use.

BEFORE STARTING TO THINK OF HOW we can embed sustainability within a brand, we need to understand how brands develop. Not all brands develop in the same way as they all have different origins, target markets, value offers, goals, etc. Knowing where they come from and how they developed over time will give us an insight into the origins of the brand as well as the other directions a brand can take. And it will give a sustainable brand a job to do.

A sustainable product will fail if you create it simply to have a positive impact on the environment. You need to think of how you develop the brand so it can create an affinity amongst customers and you need to consider how the product will be successfully used by them. It needs a job to do and it needs a brand identity to love. Sustainable brands thrive or die by the same rules as any other brand.

To help us understand these rules we need to look into the origins of brands. The origins of a brand can be traced back to four main categories. Belz and Peattie (2009) identify four main options for brand development (Table 2).

TABLE 2. Brand development

		Product category	
		Existing	New
Brand name	Existing	Line extension	Brand extension
	New	Multi-brands	New brand

2. Line extension

Line extension occurs when a company adds a new product or products of the same product category under the same brand name. This happens regularly with popular brands. Companies are constantly looking for new ways to increase market share, grow markets and/or create new revenue. Using the equity that an existing brand has developed over time is a prime opportunity to achieve any of these goals.

Some of the most successful brands have done line extensions to their product lineup. For example, the success of the Dove brand over the last

CREATING A SUSTAINABLE BRAND:
A GUIDE TO GROWING THE SUSTAINABILITY TOP LINE

10 years or so is characterized, amongst many things, by new products in their soap bar lineup. What started as a simple white soap bar has grown into a product lineup that caters for their growing line of brand supporters. The lineup now includes product varieties such as Pink Beauty Bar, Sensitive Skin Unscented Beauty Bar, Winter Care Beauty Bar, Summer Care Beauty Bar, Gentle Exfoliating Beauty Bar, the *go fresh* beauty bar options and, of course my personal favorite, Purely Pampering Coconut Milk Beauty Bar with Jasmine Petals. And we haven't even touched on the 15+ body wash products or the multiple soap bars specifically aimed at men. Line extensions to a popular brand allow companies to personalize their products to build a deeper relationship with their customers.

And Dove is not the only brand doing this. Think of Levi's that started off with 501s; Johnnie Walker and all their different labels; Glade and all the ways they bring fragrances to homes; Coca-Cola and the variety of tastes under the Coke brand; the iPhone and all the numbers, letters and colors that keeps on growing, etc. Heck, I am writing this on a HP laptop EliteBook 2570p – just one of many in their laptop range. Line extensions are the bread and butter of successful brands and expect a new version of your favorite product to come your way soon.

Line extensions can help a sustainable brand as it either uses sustainability to extend the line of a conventional product or creates an extended line of products aligned with sustainability. This way it can help companies try to counter emerging and fast-growing competitor brands by creating their own sustainable product or create new lines of revenue by offering consumers a new line of products to buy – or do a bit of both.

For instance, in 2005 Nestlé launched the Nescafé Partners' Blend (http://goo.gl/Joiyn) to both counter the negative fallout from the Oxfam

Coffee Campaign as well as make use of the fast-growing Fairtrade coffee market. This was a vast difference from their historic position of not guaranteeing farmers a minimum price for their coffee but the reputation gain and potential market growth share created a business opportunity to add new value to an existing brand by using the opportunity created by sustainability.

One of the most successful line extensions in the sustainable vehicle category can be seen in the Prius line extension which includes the 'old' Prius, the smaller Prius *C* aimed at the younger city crowd, the Prius *V* offering something for larger families, and the Prius plug-in for the fast-growing crowd who want an electric vehicle as an option.

And the genius of Anita Roddick wasn't just that she created a successful business in The Body Shop but that the business grew by introducing new line extensions that showed that a sustainable brand can be as sexy and innovative as any other mainstream company.

There are very simple reasons for brands to do this and for consumers to support this. Once we consumers know that we can trust it on one thing, it is a shortcut to trust the brand on others. Thus, we argue, 'if they got it right on sustainable bananas, they must be getting it right on avocados'. Brands can build on the positive experiences we've had and the trust we've developed in them. They get their license to extend from us.

Companies are wary that line extensions could devalue their existing products. No doubt there is some cannibalization that takes place but it also widens the overall customer base. As mentioned earlier, Dove, Levi's, Glade, Coca-Cola, Johnnie Walker, iPhone and HP all extended their brand's product lines without harming the brand – in fact, it added value to the brand. No one thought Pepsi was harming its brand when it created Diet Pepsi, Pepsi Max and Pepsi Next followed by the marketing message that it is better for you. It did not move buyers from Pepsi to Diet Pepsi but rather created new growth opportunities, identified by looking at shifts in consumer behavior. It's the same reason why they created Pepsi Throwback in the USA – new market growth opportunities.

Line extensions of the brand are to cater for changing consumer behavior and to counter other products who might aim at a specific segment of the brand consumer. It is a reaction to consumer needs and behavior and provides them with new options. Providing these options to the consumer can strengthen the value of a brand in many ways. It shows that the company is responding to consumer needs and creates a new market. Sustainability can do the same – using sustainability in line extension must show how the company is responding to the shifting consumer needs or help counter or protect against competing products and brands. It gives sustainability a job and brings tangible business benefits – it makes it sustainable.

3. Brand extension

Brand extension occurs when a company introduces product(s) into a new product category but under an existing brand name. They do it for the same reasons they extend the product lines of a brand – to use the existing brand equity to grow revenue.

Companies do this regularly. Ferrari isn't just a motor vehicle manufacturer anymore. You want a Ferrari key ring, jacket, watch, gloves, shoes and sunglasses to go with the wind blowing in your hair while driving with the top down? Or maybe you can't afford the real thing and will settle for a toy car or a t-shirt? Or, heaven forbid, a nice Ferrari red and branded stroller for your baby or Coco your little Chihuahua angel? Or maybe you are more like me who likes to mix a boyhood dream with a sustainability twist and you settle on a Ferrari travel mug.

Starbucks have grown from a series of café-style coffee shops that developed line extensions in coffee and tea to entering new product categories supporting their continued growth. Not only will you find products directly related to coffee and tea like travel mugs, coffee machines, syrups and pastries but you can buy music, books, those pesky iPhone covers and, of course, the standard bragging tool, the t-shirt, and much, much more. These are all ways to both help strengthen the brand as well as help support the growth of the company.

The world of brands is riddled with brand extension that helps strengthen consumer loyalty and affinity. My father-in-law would love to have a Johnnie Walker golf bag to go with his Johnnie Walker Black. My oldest daughter would love a beautiful blue case for her iPhone 5. And a red one and a yellow one and a beige one. . . And don't forget the speakers and dock to turn the iPhone into music heaven. My wife would love a Veuve Clicquot beach umbrella for our garden. And my youngest daughter will take anything One Direction puts on clothing, watches, sunglasses, perfume and stationery and would consider the music as a bonus. I'm just as guilty with my Levi's wallet and Timberland bag.

This is just as common amongst brands that have sustainability embedded in their value proposition. Method and Seventh Generation not only extended their product line but entered new product categories to build on their brand success. They now offer anything from kitchen and bathroom cleaner to personal care products and even baby products.

Each one of these builds on the brand equity of the original product line and develops new revenue streams that help the company grow that often forgotten third pillar of sustainability – profits.

TOMS started off with the simple concept of one-for-one – donating a pair of shoes for every pair sold. Yes they have grown their product lines by offering flats, wedges, sandals and boots for women in addition to the classic style of shoes – and men have more options too. But they have also gone beyond shoes, to offer eyewear as well on the same one-for-one principle. They have taken it even further by using their brand equity to offer a new online marketplace, called the Marketplace, to bring a vast new range of sustainable products from other sustainable brands to their growing posse of consumers and advocates. You can buy jewelry, apparel, kitchenware, headphones and so much more from brands such as Cleobella, Apolis, Falling Whistles and many more. You can even match your product with the cause and country you want to benefit and buy from. They've continued this brand extension trend by bringing in a whole new product line – coffee (**http://goo.gl/suoSXc**). Same principle but linked to water with every cup of coffee sold.

Brand extension can help sustainable brands drive into new growth areas. The same rules apply for all strong brands no matter how deep or shallow they are in the sustainability field. Learning from how conventional brands extend their brands allows sustainable brands to find new growth opportunities, reach new consumer groups and deepen brand loyalty and affinity.

4. Multi-brands

Multi-brands occur when a company has two or more brands in the same product category. This happens often with large holding companies. They either buy existing brands or create their own additional brands if they focus on a specific broad product category.

For example, Starbucks owns both Starbucks Coffee and Seattle's Best Coffee. Levi Strauss & Company owns both Levi's and Dockers. Nestlé owns Aero, Kit Kat, Smarties and Wonka in chocolate brands, Nestle Pure Life, Poland Springs, Perrier, San Pellegrino in bottled water brands. In short, multiple brands in the same product categories are a common occurrence. This is nothing new as the brands are all positioned differently and target different consumer segments – offering 'personalized' solutions and brands to fit their needs. And, of course, it happens when large holding companies decide to focus on a specific industry such as food or apparel where the consumers' choices and needs are diverse. Multi-brands allow companies to strengthen their position within the specific industry.

Sometimes companies will have two or more brands in a product category with one a brand with specific sustainability attributes. Companies do this to hedge their bets and to try and benefit from the emerging consumer demand for sustainable products. For example, Clorox has a separate brand, Green Works, focusing on bringing sustainable products to consumers in the cleaning and disinfectant product category.

Of course motor vehicle manufacturers are renowned for having multiple brands and some with a sustainability slant. Toyota has many brands competing in the marketplace and some of them compete with their Prius brand. The same for Honda and their Insight hybrid and plug-in. And Ford with their multiple sub-brands to highlight the sustainability aspects of some brand offers.

Many of the large retail chains like Safeway, Marks & Spencer, Whole Foods and Sainsbury's have their own labels that bring their customers different brand options within product categories. For example, Safeway offer organic dairy products under their O brand while offering similar non-organic dairy products under the Lucerne brand.

Even brands with a level of sustainability already attached to them will offer very specific additional sustainability sub-brands that compete with their mainstream brands. For example, Timberland's Earthkeepers brand competes with their other footwear offerings. Levi's offer Water<Less branded versions of their popular jeans and Starbucks offer a branded Fairtrade coffee in addition to their other brands.

We can expect this trend of multi-brands to continue as companies try to address consumer demands and adapt to the increasing competition from sustainable brands. And sustainable brands can strengthen their hold on a specific product category by developing multi-brands.

5. New brands

New brands occur when a company creates an entire new brand when they access a new product category or sometimes in the same product category. There are two ways this can happen – either a new brand is created for entering a new product category or a completely new product category is created thanks to the product and brand.

There are very few examples of brands that created a new product category. The reason is obvious – you only have so many new product categories. And many of the original brands didn't start off as a brand but as an idea. The Wright brothers created a new product category in flight but not a brand to go with the product category. There are many claims about who made the first ever American hamburger (**http://goo. gl/bH4h**)– some believe it was Louis Lassen while others believe it might have been Charlie Nagreen or Oscar Weber Bilby. But no one will doubt that McDonald's is known for the hamburger and the fast food industry as we know it today.

Similarly, very few will recall the first ever motorized vehicle with an internal combustion engine – the Niépces' Pyréolophore wasn't made for the mass market. Even though Karl Benz might be better known as the inventor of the modern automobile, it wasn't until Henry Ford mastered mass production in 1914 that we can truly say the product category was born and moved from a luxury product to the mass market. And, of course, soft drinks had a long history as local flavors and soda fountains before Dr Pepper was invented in 1885 and Coca-Cola in 1886. The rest is history.

There are many reasons why new brands became successful but the one thing they have in common is that they developed a product and brand presence that people wanted and continue to enjoy even though they might not have been the first mover and shaker in the field.

New brand development is also a common way for sustainability to come to life in a brand. They see an existing product category they believe isn't sustainable enough and create a brand they believe can transform the product category. And it happens in two ways. Either a new company creates a new brand or an existing company creates a new brand.

For instance, Tesla entered the motor vehicle product category with a revolutionary new solution to energy efficient vehicles. What started as a cool little car for the stars has become an increasingly high-end but mainstream product. Their growth has been phenomenal – from an idea in 2003 to an ever expanding global company (**http://goo.gl/liQ8g**). Their story is so powerful and grabbed the attention of consumers who have supported them passionately and in the way that is most important for a company – with their wallets. And others have taken notice too. Those competitors are trying everything to stop them being sold (**http:// goo.gl/EUyn**).

One of the first to react to the new development of these new brands was Skechers with their Bobs range to counter TOMS. It is a carbon copy of TOMS that links the sale of a pair of shoes to the donation of a pair of shoes to those in need. But it isn't just Skechers who copied what TOMS did. Warby Parker did the same with eyewear, WeWood does it with watches, Two Degrees does it with food bars, Roma Boots does it with rain boots, Bogobrush does it with toothbrushes and many more in the one-for-one business model.

The world of consumer goods is littered with new brands that bring a new element of sustainability to the product category. Pants to Poverty and Nudie Jeans are leading edge and the right mix of sexy apparel brands closely linking sustainability to their brand value in the same way that Theo's and Green & Black's have challenged the traditional chocolate brands. This is one of the most exciting developments – the transformation of product categories.

And don't think they are small niche little brands anymore. Whole Foods and The Body Shop aren't that small anymore. TOMS, Seventh Generation and Stonyfield Farms are no longer little startup companies with a good idea and a bit of heart. They are becoming mainstream and changing product categories and brands in new and wonderful ways.

THE BIRTH OF
A BRAND

Think of how the Prius brand has transformed the motor vehicle industry. Yes, it played in the motor vehicle manufacturing product category but it has made hybrid cars mainstream and even brought an appropriate level of sexy to the geeks in us. Every car manufacturer has been trying to cash in but most are playing catchup. Heck, Tesla is already transforming the motor vehicle industry even further by challenging traditional views on what performance and status looks like in these clean energy vehicles.

We can expect this trend of new sustainable brands in conventional product categories to continue and gather even more steam as new sustainable brands challenge the conventional brands in every product category – from food, clothing, beauty products, motor vehicles and cleaning products to new emerging sustainable brand options in technology, toys, hardware, gardening and everything else we buy and consume in today's world. Look out world of mainstream brands – be ready to be challenged. And get ready to develop your own alternative brands. We know you will.

Nothing has captured the potential of growth in this intersection between new sustainability brands and product development in recent times like those brands in the sharing economy. These new brands have created a whole new set of product categories and new ways of doing business. It has embraced the new digital world of being social and connected and found new ways to create social and/or environmental benefits through their business model. Airbnb redefined how we stay when we travel and is the poster child of the collaborative consumption movement. SideCar is challenging our world of car ownership by making catching a lift with a stranger safe and fun – and saving you money. Yerlde is making consumption of anything and how we barter and trade a whole new community game of fun. DogVacay, TaskRabbit, Uber, Lyft, Liquid, Zaarly, Lending Club, MeetMeals and SnapGoods are just a few brands in the fast-growing world of the sharing economy. Brands that didn't exist a few years back are now at the leading edge of providing products and services people use daily. And more importantly, they are becoming the new go-to brands for cool. Watch this space.

Whether it is new brands or old brands, or new product categories or old, understanding brand development helps us understand the market and how the brand can play in the marketplace. It helps the brand find its place in the world. It is an anchor and provides the heritage and authenticity needed to survive in the competitive marketplace. Knowing where you belong gives you a sense of where you are going. And, of course, it gives you a sense of all the different options open to you and the brand as you look forward to building on your success and focus on how to grow the company, sustainably.

Knowing where the brand and product comes from and where it belongs is only one part of the story. We also need to know how sustainability fits into the brand and product itself to get to a sustainable brand. What I've painted so far is a world of black and white – you are either a sustainable brand or not. But the world doesn't work that way. The beauty of sustainability is that it can come to life in many different ways in a brand. How it is embedded and the value it brings to a brand varies dramatically. What matters next is knowing that the way to embed sustainability into a brand plays according to the same rules as any other part of the value proposition of the brand. Sustainability is just one of many brand value propositions. Yes, an increasingly important value proposition as price and quality become marginal differentiators in a competitive marketplace. This is what we will focus on next – the different ways we can bring sustainability to life as we build a sustainable brand – how to embed a unique sustainability value in the brand and product. This provides a unique flavor and differentiates a sustainable brand from others in the marketplace. It brings life to your sustainable brand.

PART 3

The Anatomy of a
Sustainable Brand

1. A touch of product and a pinch of brand

THE INTERACTION BETWEEN PRODUCT and branding plays a crucial role in determining a sustainable brand. A sustainable brand cannot exist if the product itself does not have any sustainability characteristics. Similarly, a sustainable product needs to differentiate in the marketplace through branding that resonates with the consumer. This is at the heart of a sustainable brand – combining the sustainability of the product and the brand to create a unique sustainable brand value proposition and identity.

2. Product sustainability

Assumption 4: Product viability
The aim of this section is to look at how sustainability plays out in a product. It does not aim to make a statement about the product itself. But we need to make a few assumptions about the product to enable a broader discussion about sustainability and product. First, we assume that product functionality exists. That is, that the

consumer understands what the product does and has a need or want for the product. Second, we will assume that the product design is such that the consumer likes it and sees value in the design as it relates to a want or need. Third, we will assume that there is a perceived product value. That is, that the consumer sees the relationship between price and quality as something reasonable and acceptable for their purchasing decision. We assume that the product has all the basic real and perceived benefits, features, functions, uses, values, etc. that a consumer will want. In short, if you have a bad product that no one understands or wants then sustainability will make very little, if any, difference in the relationship between the product and the consumer.

This book is not going to attempt to tell you how to create a sustainable product. That will take a whole new book. There are many tools out there to help develop a sustainable product. At the very least you need to cut the fluff out when developing a sustainability product and having full product transparency will enable a more efficient way to assess product sustainability. And a great place to start figuring out how to get to product transparency is Ramon Arratia's DōShort book *Full Product Transparency* (**http://www. dosustainability.com/shop/full-product-transparency-p-11.html**).

However, we do need to understand product sustainability if we want to know how to build a sustainable brand that consumers will love and buy.

We could look at the sustainability ratings and awards to determine if a specific product is a sustainable product or not. There are numerous challenges with this approach. First, most rankings or awards are company focused and not product specific. Furthermore, awards and rankings are notoriously biased, based on their own set of criteria. I've always been skeptical about CSR rankings and ratings (**http://goo.gl/Hbl10I**), partly because there are just so many of them. It sometimes feels as if we have a ranking and rating system for every company. Just find the one that fits your needs and away you go! But this also underlines a deeper problem with rankings and ratings: is it even possible to have a ranking or rating system capture all the differences and diversity amongst companies?

There are a number of problems I have with the existing systems of rankings and ratings in determining if a product is sustainable or not:

1. **Industry differences:** The differences between industries are hardly even acknowledged but fundamental if we want to judge if a product leaves the world in a better place for future generations. Even if we limit our judgment to products and not services, the manufacturing or extraction differences are too steep to make a single standard rating workable. Most rating systems look at the impact of the manufacturing process – environmental impact, workplace practices, financial performance, community involvement, governance, etc. Nothing wrong with the criteria used – from GRI to DJSI and beyond. All robust ways to measure the impact on how a product is created. Most companies within manufacturing can be judged according to these, right? Well, just hang on for a minute there...

2. **Process vs product:** What most of these rating systems focus on, measure and rate are the impact of the process and not the impact of the actual product delivered by the manufacturing process. For example, it is possible for a tobacco company to

have excellent CSR practices in their manufacturing process and therefore rank better than, say, a pharmaceutical company. They can pay farmers a decent price, have independent certification throughout their supply chain, be highly unionized and pay the best salaries possible, and provide benefits to their employees that go beyond what anyone else ask them. But the actual product delivered by the pharmaceutical company is vastly different than those of a tobacco company – the one contributes to the health of society and the other does the opposite.

Now it will be easy to exclude tobacco companies – and many do. However, the basic principle remains. The extremes are easy to differentiate – and we can exclude tobacco and arms manufacturers. But what about comparing the products of an oil company to a pharmaceutical company? How do we judge the end product and the impact of that end product, especially when we start bringing in the idea of sustainability – leaving the future world in a better or no worse place? How do you rate a product that positions us better for the future against a company who serves an immediate need but at a much higher environmental and sustainability cost? How do you rate a software company who connects sustainable solutions to a company whose software is used for warfare? The differences in what the products deliver become complicated and make comparisons extremely difficult and challenging and almost impossible.

3. **Shared value:** The approach to ratings undermines a key development in sustainability over the last few years – finding the opportunity of mutual responsibility or shared value between the

company and its stakeholders (or society at large). Most rating systems don't allow for this to be reflected because they focus on the impact of operations and not the product impact. You can (and will) therefore have companies who practice sustainability the old way (ticking boxes, compliance, etc.) have a higher rating than companies who seek new ways to create product and service solutions that will benefit both society and the business itself. Too many ratings take a 'tick the box' approach instead of looking at innovation, opportunity, mutual responsibility, societal benefit, etc.

4. **Standardization:** The drive towards a common standard has another unwanted impact – individual criteria might mean a company has an excellent rating on some but fails on others. Let's say a company rates highly on governance, philanthropy, financial performance and the environment but their major impact is actually on human rights. And let's say this company then operates in countries where child labor or forced labor exists. The fact that they have great ratings in all but one will most likely give them a good rating overall. But they fail in the area that matters most to their specific company as it intersects with society. The standardization of ratings therefore fails to acknowledge the area of major responsibility and impact of the company – it places equal importance on all performance areas versus weighting those with greater social and/or environmental impact.

These are the biggest challenges in using ratings and rankings to determine whether a product is sustainable or not. They focus too much on the process and standardization and too little on the impact and value of the actual products and those areas of major impact and responsibility.

THE ANATOMY OF
A SUSTAINABLE BRAND

A single standard rating and ranking to compare all companies cannot capture these differences adequately. Rankings and ratings go for the lowest common denominator and fail to rate truly those who benefit society today and tomorrow and fail to acknowledge the differences in impact between different industries – or even different companies within an industry.

The model I propose to use in developing the sustainable product aspect of developing a sustainable brand focuses on two sets of criteria: the impact a product has through its value chain and the inherent value of the product itself.

1. **Value chain impact:** The value chain impact looks at the social, environmental and economic impact of a product in its creation and life in the marketplace, from sourcing to manufacturing to transport to the marketplace to post-consumer. Everything that it takes to bring a product to life and through to the end of the product life. Simply put, assessing the impact via a product life cycle assessment. Not all products are created equally. For instance, sourcing diamonds through the Kimberley Process follows established legislation and monitoring that regulates diamond mining, importing and exporting. The goal is to make the diamond trade more transparent. It might not be perfect, but it is much better than the alternative where 'conflict diamonds' can be easily smuggled across borders and over oceans to disguise their true origins, supporting and stimulating conflict. The same can be said of how apparel is manufactured, palm oil sourced, oil extracted, etc. The value chain impact will be vastly different depending on the way it is sourced and manufactured.

2. **Inherent value impact:** The second part of the model looks at the inherent value of the product itself. The question it tries to answer is whether a product creates a positive or negative good and what is the long-term impact of the product. Does it help address a key sustainability need of the world or is it a product that is a luxury or driven by want and greed? It might look like I am making a value judgment here but that is not the aim. The inherent value impact part of the product sustainability analysis is very simply a question of whether the product helps us live more sustainable lives or not. For instance, renewable energy and fossil fuels both provide us with essential products. One of them is a negative good in the long run because of the impact on climate change, health, dependency, conflict, etc. while the other addresses many of those negative impacts – it leaves us with a positive good.

Of course this is as true of services as products. In this book we use the term *products* but only because it would be cumbersome constantly to write products/services. But services should also be judged by both how they were created (the value chain impact) as well as the consequences of the service itself (the inherent value impact). For instance, a financial services company can be well managed with a strong governance structure – and even address salaries and bonuses in a way that gets the support from the Occupy movement and governments. It can even have strong community programs, great environmental initiatives and an employee volunteering program. However, if they use their key product – money – to finance mountaintop mining or conflict mining or lend money irresponsibly then the impact of their product is a negative good.

Conversely, just because a product delivers a positive good does not mean that is a sustainable product. You can create a wind turbine by using slave labor, conflict minerals and dodging taxes. That makes the product itself of great value to society but the value chain impact is horrendous.

Similarly, shared value, where companies focus on growth opportunities by tackling social problems as core business objectives, are no guarantee of a sustainable product either. Just because a product finds a shared value proposition in its interaction between the product and society doesn't mean it is a sustainable product. A product can focus on the shared value intersection with society but still have a negative impact because of their overall product impact. (Similarly, shared value tells us nothing of the brand itself – only about a program of shared value that may or may not have brand value.)

The model below attempts to create an easy way to evaluate a product's sustainability based on these two elements – the value chain impact of a product and the inherent value impact of the same product.

FIGURE 1. Product sustainability.

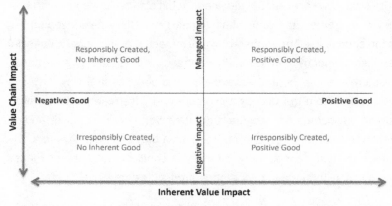

This model allows us to determine the overall sustainability of a product and how it can improve. It will also highlight the inherent limitations of that product.

Knowing these limitations is important as consumers and activists regularly accuse companies of greenwashing. Yes, this can be because of communications and brand positioning but it is just as often because the company will highlight how a product was sourced or created and ignore the inherent negative impact of the product. For example, taking another shot at the easy target of tobacco: any cigarette company can create a product by developing some form of Fairtrade sourcing of tobacco, manufacture using the best and latest Social Accountability International standard, launch a huge recycling initiative targeting the box, and be free of animal testing, etc. You think this is farfetched? Think again, an 'ethically sourced' cigarette (**http://goo.gl/cjUwR4**) was launched by 1st Nation in the UK in 2007. No one was surprised by all the negative publicity and reactions to this product. The product might be created using the latest and greatest in sustainable sourcing and manufacturing but the end product still kills.

Similarly, consumers instinctively know that solar power will always be an environmentally friendlier product than coal – no matter how clean the coal claims to be. The same way that most people instinctively know that a diet of fruit and vegetables will be more beneficial to the health of the average person than fast food hamburgers and fries. Or that a hybrid car will be better for the environment than a gas-guzzling SUV.

However, the product world isn't always that clear cut when it comes to the benefits of a product. A hybrid might be friendlier than a gas-guzzler but still not as good as a bicycle. But a bicycle has severe other limitations in the modern world. Similarly, LEDs and CFLs are better than the old light bulbs but maybe not as good as a candle. The candle just isn't fit for a modern lifestyle and therefore not truly a sustainable product when using the people, planet and profit triple bottom line approach.

What kind of products are those which will rank the highest in the inherent value impact? It will be the products that were created to deal with specific sustainability challenges or offer unique sustainable alternatives to fit our modern lifestyle: for example, wind turbines and solar power to harness renewable energy sources, Fairtrade and Marine Stewardship Council certified products, 'green' cleaning products, LEDs and CFLs, hybrid and electric cars, healthy and organic foods, etc.

On the flip side will be the extremes such as tobacco that will have a negative impact on people's health, guns and ammunition for obvious reasons, 'blood diamonds' sourced from and financing conflicts and wars, food with unhealthy levels of sugar, salt or fat, products with high emissions of carbon or CFCs, etc.

Most products will fall somewhere closer to the middle. We will have to judge each product on its own when using this model. Think of where a pair of Timberland Earthkeepers will fall compared to a pair of TOMS. Or where any of those two will fall compared to the knock-off sold on the streets in NY? Some are easy to determine and some a little bit more complicated.

This model allows us to determine one component of a sustainable brand – the product side. The flipside is looking at how sustainability is embedded into the branding of a product.

3. Sustainability branding

Brands can't be boring. Or rather, successful brands need to differentiate in the marketplace and can't lead from the middle. The same rules apply when building a sustainable brand – it needs to grab the attention of the consumer.

Brands come to life in two very simple ways – how they align with the interest and values of the consumer to offer a unique value that the consumer will buy into and how they disrupt the marketplace to create interest and attention amongst consumers.

Sustainability branding is a different approach from the product sustainability approach as it isn't about its material impact. In product sustainability a product can have a negative or positive side. In other words, a product can simply be bad in every aspect – from how it is made to how the product itself impacts the world. Branding is about how the brand comes to life in the marketplace and how values and value comes to life in the brand. Yes, there can be bad branding but that has minimal material impact on the world. We are more interested in how the values are embedded and how the brand comes to life in the marketplace.

The **brand impact** is how brands create a presence in the marketplace. Some brands take the marketplace by storm through the branding of a new innovative product or brand positioning. Think of some of the most disruptive brands in the world today. One could argue that Apple is a brand that developed slowly over time but the iPhone, iPod and iPad have transformed the marketplace in the blink of an eye. The product innovations associated with these brands are only one aspect of the success story. The army of devoted Apple disciples has gone beyond the typical fan boy devotion and is bordering on an addiction mentality. The launches of these products, the secrecy associated with product development, fans addiction to any news or updates, the amount of news and magazine space dedicated to anything Apple and everything else that goes around the Apple brands and their devoted supporters have taken the disruption that brands can cause to a whole new level. But how did Apple do this? Very simply by focusing on the demand side – the consumer. In essence, consumers, their emerging needs, their wants and desires, their quest for a better life; and everything that goes into them buying a product or not. It went beyond simple design and pricing. Apple developed these various attributes to 'seduce' the consumer's mind and address their anxieties and emotions. This is key to understanding the Apple innovation. It wasn't just in terms of the technology, but also in terms of the value the product offers consumers, the advantages it has over conventional competing products and the gap it fills in their lives. That was the disruption of the Apple brand.

The Apple brand created disruption in both how it was positioned with consumers as well as the way it came to life through the launch and product experience. These two elements are key in understanding the impact of a brand:

1. **Messaging:** The story and narrative of the brand. It tells us what is unique to the brand and why each consumer will or should care. It makes it personal and gives the brand an identity. Brands create these messages and brand attributes to connect with their targeted consumer and to build loyalty, affinity, love, trust, etc. between the brand and the consumer.

2. **Medium:** If the messaging is the 'saying' part then the medium

is the 'doing' part. This is where the brand comes into action. It can be wild ways to launch a product or more traditional in how it engages the consumer.

Think of these two elements of the brand impact as how the brand starts dating the consumer. The messaging will tell the consumer who the brand is – its life, where it lives, what it likes, etc. The medium is dating itself – the places where they will go and the things they will do.

Brands differ in how they create the brand impact and what they emphasize. For instance, most motor vehicle companies focus on the messaging. They build a narrative that they hope their target audience will embrace and make them fall in love with a specific vehicle. The reason is clear, the competitive set and the reason for car purchasing is fairly well established. The places where consumers go to make their decisions are well established so the ability for a motor vehicle company to find a new medium to engage the consumer is limited. They focus on how to differentiate in the messaging – comfort or sporty, fuel efficient or power, family or fun, etc.

On the other hand, the tech industry is littered with brands that change how we interact with brands – the medium. Snapchat, Pinterest, Go-Pro, Netflix, Hulu, Facebook, Twitter, Vine and everything in between has changed how we interact with brands. Their rise is fast and their impact disruptive.

Each brand will decide on the right balance and that will determine their brand impact:

- **Disruptive**: Brands that are both strong in message and medium tend to be disruptive as their messaging is supported by cutting-edge execution.

- **Engaging:** Brands that focus on the message more than medium tend to be more reserved and aim at building a consistent and lasting brand and brand experience. Brands that focus on the medium more than messaging tend to be highly engaging brands that try to catch the consumer's attention through eye-catching tactics while the messaging plays a supporting role.

- **Incremental:** And, of course, some brands keep a very low profile on both sides and tend to be more incremental – a steady as she goes approach to brand impact.

Brands in the sustainability space use the disruptive approach to break through the conventional marketplace and build strong consumer relations. TOMS grabbed the attention of the consumer by challenging the traditional ways that consumers could interact with the brand and product. They weren't just selling shoes anymore but were selling a lifestyle. They made the consumer part of the solution and part of the story of the brand. Without the consumer involvement there was no product and no brand. Yes, every product needs a consumer to buy them but TOMS took it to a new level by making the sustainability promise of the brand central to the relationship with the consumer. But they not only had a very strong message – they backed it up by using innovative ways to connect to the consumer (the medium). They combined traditional and online media and made heavy use of social media to grow awareness and consumer support.

Dove used a more engaging way to create brand impact. Although well established, they nevertheless transformed the brand by taking a hugely disruptive approach to redefining the messaging of the brand through their Campaign for Real Beauty. However, the mediums used were more reserved and more in line with the beauty product category.

CREATING A SUSTAINABLE BRAND:
A GUIDE TO GROWING THE SUSTAINABILITY TOP LINE

Some of the leading-edge sustainability brands have taken a disruptive approach to both the message and the medium. These companies have embraced their sustainability roots and even weaknesses to create disruptive campaigns in the marketplace that grabbed consumer attention. Patagonia's Don't Buy This Jacket (**http://goo.gl/saa4le**) campaign created a stir when it launched by asking people to not buy the environmentally unfriendly Patagonia jacket. Chipotle's Scarecrow campaign (**http://goo.gl/v4fMni**) tackled factory farming as part of their drive to highlight the challenges in the fast food industry. They supported this with a game, advertising, research, social media, traditional media, etc., combining a very powerful message with a series of disruptive tactics that captured the imagination.

But not all brands are disruptive or engaging. Some brands take a more incremental approach and create slow and steady change. You would think that in this hyper-connected world a slow build over time, easing into the marketplace, would become increasingly challenging. But this isn't the case at all. Many brands ease into changes through incremental and small changes. This often happens with established brands with an established consumer market and where disruption can easily create an unwanted consumer backlash.

Think of Coca-Cola who is seen as a steady and established brand. The brand is still one of the most valuable brands in the global market. Apple might be the top global brand according to Interbrand but Coca-Cola remains a power player in the Top 5 (**http://goo.gl/DA9Xy9**). It's not just Interbrand that thinks so, Millward Brown's annual BrandZ (**http://goo.gl/wtviM**) that ranks the Top 100 Most Valuable Brands also puts Coca-Cola in the Top 5. Steady and incremental growth in the brand value.

Yes, every now and again they will launch a new Coca-Cola brand like Diet Coke, Coca-Cola Zero, Cherry Coke or Coca-Cola Black Zero Vanilla – that's a mouthful. But they tend to stay away from disruptive changes and rightly so. Incremental changes like adding a caffeine-free or diet version of the popular Coke is fine as long as it doesn't change the original brand.

Many brands use this same incremental approach to build their sustainability offering to the consumer. What might have started as a simple brand like Method has changed from a simple line of products such as dish soap to a wide range of branded Method products that include bathroom cleaners, kitchen cleaners, hand soap, pet clean-up kits, laundry detergent, dishwasher tabs, wood polish and many more brand extensions. None of these were disruptive but slowly and surely changed the marketplace in incremental ways. It allows brands to reduce risks and test the marketplace without major capital outlay.

The challenge today is that we live in a connected world where consumers are flooded with information and attention spans are shorter than ever before. The incremental approach to creating breakthrough and consumer interest is more challenging today than ever before. Edelman's Trust Barometer (**http://goo.gl/gKZ7HU**) shows that Millennials don't trust companies or the information they see in the same way as their parents: 64% of them need to hear information three to five times before they believe it. And another 12% need to hear it 10 or more times! But the problem is even more complex than expected as they need to hear it from different sources. Online search is more trusted than any other information source. In fact, social media (**http://goo.gl/PV58T6**) is essential in all engagement with them and that has influenced not only how they consume information but also where. So not only do they need to hear it many times but they need to hear and see it from many sources, places and people. It has changed the old ways that trust in brands were developed, from traditional marketing and advertising to new ways of interacting with those brands and how they build band affinity and loyalty.

The rules have changed and the competing interests, flood of information and information sources and new consumer expectations require brands to be more disruptive to break through the noise and clutter. Of course it will have to be relevant to the brand identity and brand value proposition but brands have to consider what disruption means for them. Brands with impact create disruption in the world of today. But a sustainable brand needs to align this brand disruption with brand relevant sustainability.

Sustainability association is the final component needed to create a sustainable brand. We've identified the sustainability of the product (or service) that determines whether a brand even stands a chance of being taken seriously. We've also looked at how a brand can create impact by being either disruptive or through an incremental approach. What is missing is how sustainability itself plays out in the brand – how it comes to life and how it aligns with the interests and values of the consumer to offer a unique value proposition that consumers will buy into. This is the final element to determine a sustainable brand – bringing sustainability to life in the brand.

Assumption 5: Branding attributes

We will assume that a brand already has key elements in place –
from the brand value proposition and attributes to brand identity,
personality and beyond. Brands need to offer the customer something
in addition to the perceived product value based only on price and
quality factors. There are many different brand attributes but key to
them is to help make a brand relevant, consistent, credible, unique
and appealing to customers. Without these attributes all brands
will fail – no matter how sustainable the product. The Management
Study Guide identifies eight attributes a strong brand should have.

BRAND ATTRIBUTES

Relevance	A brand must be relevant. It must meet people's expectations and should perform the way they want it to.
Consistency	A brand must be consistent if customers are to believe in the brand. A consistent brand is where the company communicates message in a way that does not deviate from the core brand proposition.
Positioning	A brand should be positioned so that it takes a place in the customer's mind and they prefer it over other brands.
Credibility	A brand should do what it promises. It should not fail to deliver what it promises.
Inspiration	A brand should inspire the category it is famous for. And it should inspire the customer.

Uniqueness	A brand should be different and unique. It should set you apart from other competitors in the market.
Appeal	A strong brand should be attractive. Customers should be attracted by the promise you make and by the value you deliver.
Sustainability	A strong brand makes a business competitive. A sustainable brand drives an organization towards continuous success.

But the attributes of a brand only tells us a part of the brand story. Each brand needs to have a brand value proposition (**http://goo.gl/sT3IwJ**) to bring it to life for the customer – a reason for them to connect to the brand. The brand value proposition is a promise that your brand must keep. It tells the customer the value the brand brings to them and connects with them on a personal level. Think of Spotify's promise that they will *Soundtrack Your Life*. Or Skype's promise that *Wherever You Are, Wherever They Are – Skype Keeps You Together*. Or The Ladder's promising that *Your Career Is Our Job*.

We will assume that these key brand attributes and brand propositions are already in place and focus on how sustainability comes to life within these existing brand distinctions – and how sustainability can add further value to these brand factors.

Sustainability can help strengthen brand loyalty amongst consumers by adding to the brand value proposition and brand identity. It can strengthen trust in the brand promise and help connect the values of the brand to the values of the customer.

However, the role and depth of sustainability in brands can vary dramatically. At one end of the spectrum sustainability can be completely absent from the brand value proposition while it can be completely embedded in the next brand. For example, the Prius has sustainability at the center of the brand and product while the Hummer never claimed to have anything connected to sustainability in its brand and value proposition.

Of course the brand world isn't that black and white. And this is especially true when it comes to how sustainability is embedded in the brand. In most cases the value proposition that sustainability offers a brand can be linked within the brand in many different ways. The framework in Table 3 highlights the ways that sustainability is associated within the brand proposition.

TABLE 3. Sustainability associated brand proposition framework

NOTE: The brands in this section are not meant to be the definitive list of brands. Some brands will feel they should be mentioned somewhere else. Some brands will feel that they are in the wrong section. So be it: not only can brands change from one section to another but, depending on the depth of knowledge, research, insights, analysis, etc., brands can potentially be placed in another section. For instance, Dove is listed under section 4 (Aligned), but can just as easily be captured under sections 6 (Enhanced) or 7 (Inspired) because the brand transformation and impact of sustainability on the brand was so radical. The aim is not perfection but rather to create better understanding.

ASSOCIATION	DESCRIPTION	EXAMPLE
1. Ignored	Complete absence of any sustainability claims or practices within the brand. The usual suspects of cigarette companies and arms & ammunition manufacturers. But also brands that do not claim or add any sustainability value or identity in their brand offer. It does not mean the brand does not have some sustainability practices but rather that they do not claim any in developing the brand identity and brand value offer. It is also not a list of the perceptions that people have of a specific brand as that list can (and will) change dramatically in a short period of time. For example, as recently as 2008 BP was rated as greener brand than Greenpeace (http://goo.gl/jd6Onw) – a claim very few people will make today. Furthermore, the brand could also fall in this category if they have taken a stand against very specific social or environmental issues or are known for specific environmental or social fallout.	• Marlboro and Smith & Wesson and the impact of the final product. • BlackRock and Peabody Energy and their involvement in coal. • Domino's Pizza & Chic-fil-A and controversy surrounding social issues (healthcare, gay rights, minimum wages). • Exxon and Koch Industries lobbying against climate change. • Snapchat and Diesel jeans with no sustainability value as part of the brand offer.

ASSOCIATION	DESCRIPTION	EXAMPLE
2. Complied	Brands who call out specific actions they have taken in reaction to criticism. These brands generally react and highlight specific actions because of activist campaigns and/or product recalls. Sustainability may or may not have played a role in their brand before but the alignment with a specific issue or issues is meant to show how they have changed or complied with acceptable practices to address these issues. These might be one-off ways the brand deals with the issue or can become part of a longer-term brand association to counter potential negative brand impacts and/or highlight the positive actions a brand takes to address sustainability issues associated with the brand.	• Coca-Cola and aluminum recycling to align with them being the world's largest user of aluminum can sheet. • McDonald's and healthy food options after sustained campaigning about their impact on obesity and their marketing to children. • Poland Springs and the Eco-Shape bottle in reaction to the anti-bottled water campaign. • BP and Gulf Coast tourism advertising to highlight their work after the Gulf oil spill. • Anheuser-Busch and responsible drinking to address concerns related to the abuse of their products.

ASSOCIATION	DESCRIPTION	EXAMPLE
3. Observed	Some brands observe the principles of sustainability. They follow best practices when implementing sustainability within the creation of the products and are generally respected for the work they do within sustainability. However, they do not always align their brand with sustainability or embed sustainability in their brand. The general sustainability they do practice tends to be accepted as part of the brand value even when they do not make it part of their branding. In this case sustainability becomes an unintentional but value-adding brand proposition. Consumers will most likely not be aware of the sustainability work of the brands or awareness will be low when compared to other brand attributes. However, the 'behind the scenes' work some of these brands do in sustainability might be well known amongst sustainability experts and peers.	• Apple often ranks as a top sustainable brand because of their general brand attributes and even though they do not position their brand as sustainable. • Mercedes Benz fuel efficiency innovations have given the brand sustainability credentials even when it is not part of the branding and positioning. • L'Oréal has built strong sustainability credentials through their sustainability work but do not align their brand with these innovations. • Other companies where sustainability has created some halo affect without the brand being aligned with a social cause or sustainability include Campbell Soup, Kellogg's, Caterpillar, adidas and Allianz.

ASSOCIATION	DESCRIPTION	EXAMPLE
4. Aligned	An early form of bringing sustainability to life for a brand has been cause branding or cause marketing. This allows a brand to align with a cause that enhances the brand value and proposition. Cause marketing and branding has changed dramatically over the years. Historically it was driven by a cause that wasn't always aligned with the brand, product, service or company. The cause itself was high on the consumer awareness scale and this created brand value through association. This has changed dramatically over the last 20 odd years where cause marketing or branding is now more closely associated with the intersection between the brand or product and the cause it wants to support.	• American Express and their 1983 Statue of Liberty Restoration campaign (**http:// goo.gl/Mpq3Ma**) was the birth of cause marketing as we know it today. • Yoplait's Save Lids to Save Lives has been one of the most successful long-running campaigns in the USA and highlights the partnership with Susan G. Komen for the Cure. • Dove Campaign For Real Beauty didn't adopt a cause but created one with breakthrough creative that sparked an international discussion of beauty stereotypes. • Citi Bank played to their roots, their name and a key environmental and social challenge when they aligned with bike sharing in New York. • The Home Depot's 1,000 Playgrounds In 1,000 Days partnership with KaBOOM aligned a key competency of the company with volunteerism and a specific outcome over a defined period of time. • Product (Red) allowed brands to align with a well-known cause, celebrities and other brands to create a larger halo effect.

ASSOCIATION	DESCRIPTION	EXAMPLE
5. Acquired	Brands can get additional brand value through sustainability by creating a unique sustainability value for their brand. In most cases these brands create a unique sustainability program or identity by using their brand proposition and identity as their unique view, implementation and alignment of sustainability. These brands do not start off with a sustainability offer but their deep brand understanding and identity enable them to acquire a unique take on sustainability that allows this to be embedded in the brand and that brings new and additional value to the brand. These brands remain true to their original value proposition and identity but have enhanced it by acquiring sustainability elements into the brand. The value and strength of this approach is that most of the brands are well established and this strength brings great value to sustainability through the association with the brand. It also helps carve out a new and unique brand distinction in a competitive marketplace for mature brands and/or protects them from perceived vulnerabilities before it becomes a major issue they need to manage.	• Nike has taken their inherent brand value and identity around design to the center of their approach to sustainability. • GE's Ecomagination is aligned with their business priorities through a commitment to build innovative solutions for today's environmental challenges while driving economic growth. • Nokia took the public need for mobility and personalization by offering an 'Eco Hero' product line as well as an 'Eco' profile for every model. • Walmart has turned criticism and vulnerability into innovation in sustainability through their focus on the impact they have through their supply chain. • IKEA is about making shopping, designing and assembly easy and effortless and they have taken this similar approach to transforming their business approach to sustainability and the consumer involvement with sustainability without the consumer being aware of it.

ASSOCIATION	DESCRIPTION	EXAMPLE
6. Enhanced	There are companies where sustainability is part and parcel of the value proposition and identity of the brand. The products may be mainstream products not meant to inspire or create a more sustainable world and they may not address any specific sustainability issues but the brand is fully aligned with the values captured through sustainability. Some of these brands had it as part of who they were from the start while others developed it over time. Values and commitment to a more sustainable world tend to be deeply rooted in these brands and their roots can typically be traced back to the founding principles or founders of the brand. These brands typically have authenticity and personal commitment deeply rooted in the brand and products.	• Levi's is all about style and coolness but their values have been the same since 1853: empathy, originality, integrity and courage – deeply rooted in sustainability. • Ben & Jerry's has made sustainability part of their ethos from the start and constantly create ice-cream flavors to reflect their sustainability commitments – such as Hubby Hubby to support gay marriage and Imagine Whirled Peace. • Unilever has transformed the brand and business proposition through their Sustainable Living plan. • Timberland took their deep-rooted commitment to sustainability to create the Earthkeepers line that has expanded throughout the brand lineup. • Companies such as Marks & Spencer, REI, The North Face, Starbucks, Eileen Fisher, Panera and Wegman's Food Market have all deepened their brand alignment with sustainability to acquire a heightened brand value proposition and identity.

ASSOCIATION	DESCRIPTION	EXAMPLE
7. Inspired	A number of brands are inspired by a specific sustainability issue or issues. These brands can trace their origin or transformation to a specific sustainability issue or issues. Sustainability is therefore deeply rooted within the brand value proposition and identity even when the product itself remains a mainstream type product. The products and brand tend to make the world a better place and their existence can be found in wanting to bring sustainability into the creation of the product and brand within a specific product category.	• TOMS was inspired by a poverty-related issue and the brand remains deeply rooted in sustainability even though the product is shoes and nothing more. • Nescafe Partners' Blend is a coffee that started because of the Oxfam Coffee Campaign but the brand exists because it tries to address specific sustainability issues related to coffee. • Chipotle was inspired by the need to create a fast casual dining experience but to do this through organic products and sustainably raised meat. • Theo's and Green & Black might be great chocolate brands but they found their inspiration in the sustainability challenges of the chocolate farmers. • Stonyfield Farms, Naked Juice, Sun Chips, Bob's of Skechers, Pants to Poverty, Warby Parker, Bogo Brush and so many other brands can find their roots in the inspiration driven by sustainability.

ASSOCIATION	DESCRIPTION	EXAMPLE
8. Designed	There are products that are specifically designed to address sustainability issues and the nature of the brand and the associated product or products are to create a more sustainable world. Almost all of these brands were created to counter the perceived negative effects of other mainstream brands and products. Some of the products started off with trying to address negative impacts of mainstream products, while others are created because the drive towards a more sustainable world has created the need for a new product or products.	• Method and Seventh Generation can both find their origins in the need to create a household brand that is good for the environment and people. • The Body Shop challenged the traditional wisdom of beauty products by not only turning it into a range of sustainable products but by using the power of the brand to advocate for social and environmental change – the first corporate activist brand. • Whole Foods created a sustainability focused brand that enabled consumers with social and environmental conscience to buy their consumer products at a retail brand who shared their values and who they could trust. • Prius transformed the hybrid vehicle market through clever branding and a unique brand proposition. • Sidecar created a unique business and brand by enabling individuals to share rides and thereby help manage the triple bottom line of sustainability – environment, social and economic.

CONTINUED OVER

ASSOCIATION	DESCRIPTION	EXAMPLE
		• Tom's of Maine, Patagonia, TerraPass, Leaf, Tesla, Green Works, Co-op, Kind, Grameen Bank, Wakawaka, Airbnb, Yerdle, Uber, Lyft, TaskRabbit, Lending Club are all brands that were designed to address sustainability challenges and their brand proposition is deeply aligned with sustainability.
		Of course most of the well-known sustainability certification scheme brands and related product brands find their roots in this section – Fairtrade, Rainforest Alliance, Marine Stewardship Council and Forest Stewardship Council.

None of the above means a brand is perfect. Perfection is not part of the sustainability agenda – or else we wouldn't need constant improvement. It provides us with a scale to assess whether sustainability association in the brand is completely absent or whether it is embedded – from ignored to designed. The table above is an easy to understand framework to help define where and how sustainability can be associated within the brand value proposition.

Of course brands do not always stay within a specific group as they are constantly adapting to new trends and adopting new practices.

But knowing where a brand falls or could fall within this framework can help in directing how to build the connection with the consumer. Knowing how sustainability is associated within the brand can help guard against accusations of greenwashing or claiming benefits or origins that were never part of the brand. And, of course, it can help a brand define and redefine sustainability within the brand value proposition as the brand continues to develop and as sustainability continues to develop over time within the brand identity.

The framework also helps us develop the sustainability branding model that looks at the intersection between the brand impact and sustainability association – the two key elements in connecting sustainability and branding.

FIGURE 2. Sustainability branding.

This model allows us to determine how sustainability branding can be created and the journey the brand is on in developing its sustainability proposition. Of course it also highlights the inherent challenges a brand will have in bringing sustainability to the brand value proposition and identity.

Understanding these challenges helps protect the brand against criticism – or at least provides a solid buffer against it. No brand is completely protected against criticism – sustainability or not. The reasons are simple: there are always personal preferences involved, simple product mistakes can have a negative brand impact, etc.. Think of one of the most loved contemporary brands, Apple – universally loved for its design and brand identity and proposition. Even Apple had recent failures with the Apple TV and even the new Apple iPhone 5C isn't a huge seller. It hasn't hurt the Apple brand much because they have brand equity that provides a buffer to soften the blow of criticism. Similarly, Timberland has a buffer of goodwill and when Greenpeace targeted them in 2008 the brand damage was minimal. Sustainability branding does not prevent brand mistakes but can help build goodwill to soften the blow.

Branding sustainability goes further than purely protection though. For some brands it drives differentiation in the marketplace. Whether gift at purchase (like Yoplait) or a purchasing driver (such as Earthkeepers or Levi's Water<Less jeans), branding sustainability can change the fortunes of a company in the marketplace. This is a fundamental difference in brands – some approach branding sustainability as a defensive mechanism while others see it as a proactive way to attract consumers.

Branding sustainability can also provide the way for sustainability to find its place within the brand proposition, brand promise and brand identity. It adds to the brand value proposition. It helps create and solidify the brand in the mind of the consumer. Sustainability branding doesn't mean that there is a sustainable brand yet. But it does mean that both elements needed for a sustainable brand have now been identified – the product sustainability and the branding sustainability. These are the two pillars of the Sustainable Brand Model.

4. The Sustainable Brand Model

Merging these two pillars of a sustainable brand – product sustainability and branding sustainability – allows us to create a model for developing a sustainable brand. The Sustainable Brand Model can be represented thus:

FIGURE 3. Sustainable Brand Model.

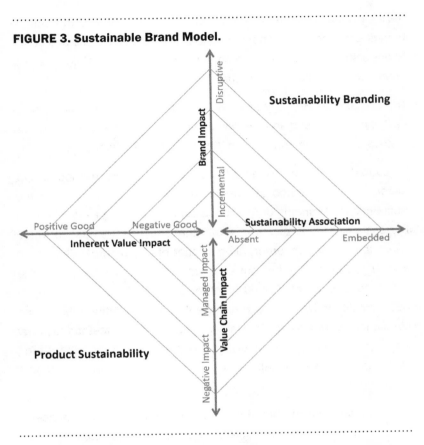

The aim is not to search for the perfect diamond or sustainable brand – that is simply not possible. The purpose of the model is to guide brands as they search for their unique sustainable brand offer. The truth is that not all brands or products are born equal. Some will be more sustainable than others. Some are limited by the nature of their products or brands while others make up for it through the rigorous discipline they use in running their sustainability strategy throughout the value chain. Furthermore, brands and products are not static. They constantly innovate and adapt to any shifts in society or if a brand or product becomes stale. In short, brands and products are by nature dynamic.

The Sustainable Brand Model helps us determine the unique offer of each individual brand and how companies can strengthen their brand as a sustainable brand and position the brand in an authentic way.

Of course it will vary from one product and brand to another. For instance, using Method as an example, we can determine that the Sustainability Branding of Method is especially strong as it relates to the *sustainability association* within the brand as well as the *value chain impact* and *inherent value impact* of the product. The *brand impact* is also strong but not as strong as the other elements. The reason for this is that Method is not the first brand within the category but their disruptive approach has created a substantial interest and consumer awareness and buy-in. This analysis allows Method to pretty much play in every aspect of a sustainable brand and the strong overall performance in all various elements has created a robust sustainable brand.

It also means that the brand identity and value proposition is deeply rooted in sustainability. It is therefore also vulnerable in case there is a product or brand flaw or risk as it relates to sustainability. For instance, the brand would be more damaged by allegations of environmental damage due to the product ingredients than a conventional cleaning product. This does not mean the brand should lower the risk associated with sustainability as all brands lean towards a specific value proposition or set of indicators. For instance, Apple is highly dependent on cutting-edge design and reducing the risk will lessen the impact of the brand overall. Method is steeped in sustainability at almost every level and reducing the risk will harm the brand identity and value proposition.

FIGURE 4. Sustainable Brand Model: Method.

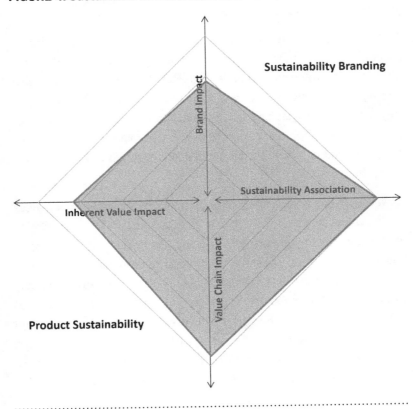

Another interesting example to look at is TOMS. They have taken the market by storm over the last few years and make for an interesting case study of the Sustainable Brand Model. They are particularly strong on both of the *sustainability branding* elements of the model. The *brand impact* has been extremely disruptive and redefined the relationship between business and addressing some of the most pressing social challenges – as captured in the numerous media and social media stories about the brand and product.

Similarly, *sustainability association* with the brand is extremely strong as their advocates and the consumer associates the social good offered with the brand value proposition and identity. The *inherent value impact* of the product is also very strong with the product benefiting society in very specific ways. It isn't perfect because of the potential negative long-term economic impact and dependency that it might create. But at its core, the product adds substantial sustainability value purely through the product itself.

However, the *sustainable brand* is undermined by an apparent weakness in the *value chain impact*. This is due to the lack of beneficiation in the manufacturing and due to a lack of a clear comprehensive sustainability strategy, compliance policies and guidelines, reporting, etc. This leaves the brand vulnerable in one key part of the Sustainable Brand Model. This is especially risky for a brand that relies heavily on their sustainability credentials to drive customer loyalty and brand awareness. The model therefore allows TOMS to make an assessment of its vulnerabilities and also brings a focus to what the benefit claims can and cannot include.

FIGURE 5. Sustainable Brand Model: TOMS.

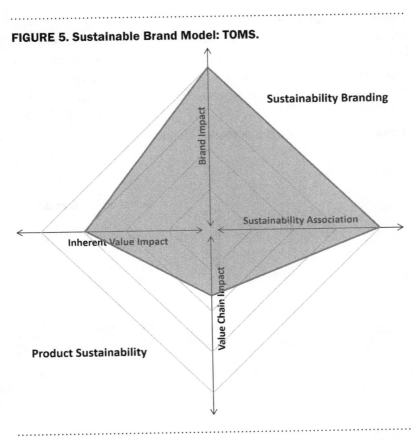

Another example is that old favorite, Marlboro. The Sustainable Brand Model identifies the inherent weaknesses associated with the brand as it relates to sustainability. The one area of relative strength, *value chain impact*, is undermined by the lack of sustainability value from a *sustainability branding* perspective and the very poor showing in the *inherent value impact*. These weaknesses undermine any attempt by

Marlboro to highlight the one area of relative strength as the critics will very quickly point out the much larger issues as they relate to sustainability in the brand and product. In this case the Sustainability Brand Model identifies the sustainability risk associated with the brand. As a result the brand will more likely highlight other perceived brand

FIGURE 6. Sustainable Brand Model: Marlboro.

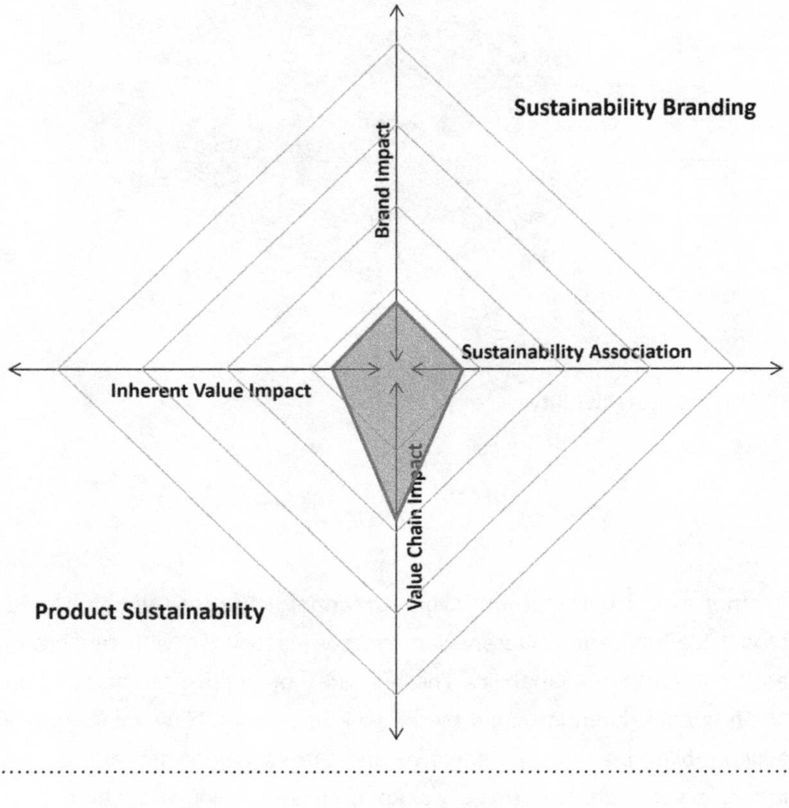

benefits, value propositions and identity when positioning the brand as sustainability will offer little value and too much risk.

Most brands do not fall within the extremes of the Sustainable Brand Model. An analysis of a more typical company such as Nokia shows that they do not have any major weaknesses or strengths associated with their Sustainable Brand Model analysis. Yes, almost all areas can improve, but because of the balance that is created amongst the four indicators, no high risk is associated with the brand as it relates to sustainability. The risk increases for the brand if it pushes a communications strategy based on any one of the indicators without substantially improving their practices in that specific area. The strongest brand value proposition of Nokia lies in other elements and not the sustainability attributes. It has enough credentials to engage their consumers and targets around sustainability and do some Sustainability Branding but not as the main value proposition or brand identity.

It does mean that the brand needs to keep a close eye on competitors to see if the competing brands might exploit sustainability elements in their brand value proposition. It also enables the brand to make regular assessments of its own brand to evaluate whether any changes allow for brand differentiations in an increasingly competitive marketplace. And, of course, it enables the brand to identify any specific areas it can target to strengthen its own sustainable brand.

....

FIGURE 7. Sustainable Brand Model: Nokia.

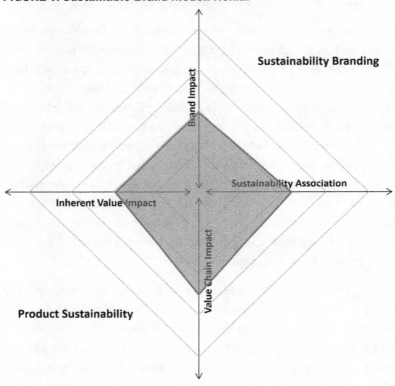

....

This model isn't the answer to everything sustainable. It doesn't guarantee that a brand is sustainable. The world of sustainability, brands, products and consumers is way too complex and dynamic for that big box to be ticked by one simple model. No, the Sustainable Brand Model is a tool that marries the two key elements of a sustainable brand together – product and brand. The model aims to simplify the complicated world of brand and product. But, more importantly, the model is meant to both deepen our understanding of what it takes to be a sustainable brand as well as be a practical tool to guide the development of a sustainable brand. There are a few ways this model can benefit companies, brands and even consumers and experts (Table 4).

TABLE 4. Key benefits of the Sustainable Brand Model

Position	Clarifies how a brand can or cannot be positioned and the inherent limitations associated with the brand
Create	Helps create a sustainable brand by mapping the key sustainability attributes
Compete	Identifies additional ways a brand and product can compete in an increasingly competitive marketplace
Risk	Helps manage and reduce the risk or risks associated with sustainability and sustainability claims
Improve	Helps measure and evaluate sustainability claims and identifies areas for improvement
Adapt	Enables brands to adapt to the ever changing sustainability landscape – from products and brands to competitors and consumers
Personalize	Identifies the unique sustainability-related brand value proposition, attributes and identity

So there you have it – the blissful married life of product and brand. A simple model to try and cut through the myriad rankings and ratings and awards that cloud the world of sustainability. A model that makes cutting through the countless product claims and brand promises uncomplicated and straightforward. Of course it isn't going to stop people from making silly claims or stupid mistakes – but at least we will now know how wrong they are and point fingers while we chuckle and shake our heads. Never mind the pesky consumers – worry more about those pesky products and brands. May they live to be a long and happy sustainable brand.

5. Final thoughts

Sustainability is no guarantee that a brand will be successful. We have to accept that products are products and brands are brands, and that the rules remain the same whether it is bringing sustainability to the brand or if it follows the conventional route. Central to all of this is innovation and with innovation comes failure. No truly cutting-edge company has hit a home run with every single release. Who remembers the Apple Newton? Kellogg's breakfast mates? Pepsi A.M.? Have you ever eaten a McDonald's Arch Delux? Or what about Kitchen Entrees by Colgate? Who owned an IBM PCjr?

More recently, who thought Qwikster was a great idea?

These companies have succeeded despite the occasional flop – and I'd venture to guess they learned a great deal from their mistakes. No one stopped investing in Apple, IBM, Ford, McDonald's, Netflix or any of the companies I've listed just because of one or two product failures. It is the nature of all business. It is in the nature of growth. And it is in the nature of innovation. A key lesson for those building a sustainable brand – get used to failure as it is inherent across every sector and simply a part of the evolutionary process of business.

What gets me isn't failures but rather the murky waters when I hear the claims of 'sustainable brands'. Both research and consumer purchasing and behavior tells us that consumers do want products that share their values and are already buying products and support brands they believe help them live more sustainable lives. Of course sustainability isn't the only or even the prime reason why most of them do buy and support these brands. It is just one of many brand value propositions. Yes, an increasingly important part of the brand value proposition but still one of many.

The challenge is that most brands haven't kept up with the changes in consumer needs and behavior. Companies will complain that consumers aren't interested in sustainable brands and then complain about increased competition from Method, Seventh Generation, Marks & Spencer, Unilever, Dove, Levi's, Timberland, Patagonia, TOMS, Whole Foods, Starbucks and all those brands who carry their values and value right on their sleeve where every single consumer can see it. Those annoying sustainable brands. . .

And that is where the second mistake comes in. Companies start bragging about their 'sustainable brand' and pitch the latest ranking, rating and awards to get the nod of approval from the experts to confirm that they too have a sustainable brand. And they can't understand that consumers don't believe them or buy into their version of a sustainable brand. The reason is very simple – a sustainable brand is more than a slap on the back and a medal.

To get to what a sustainable brand is we need to go look at the dance between the product and the brand. But before we can dance we need to know that the sustainability of products needs to look at both how it is made and the impact of the product itself – how it got here and what the impact is now that it is here. Eureka! We now know what it takes to be a sustainable product! And the same dual approach goes for the brand. We need to know how sustainability comes to life in the action it takes and the stories it tells, as well as how deep (or not) sustainability is embedded into the brand value proposition and identity. Kapow! Sustainability branding!

The sustainable product and sustainability branding are the yin-yang of a sustainable brand. You can't have one and none of the other. The Sustainable Brand Model provides a way for us to evaluate the claims made by brands as well as provide brands with a tool to get closer to that elusive sustainable brand status. No brand is perfect, but the model is a guide to get brands a little bit closer to where they need to be to make people stop laughing and start buying.

So the next time you hear companies complain that consumers aren't there yet – point and laugh as they are missing the boat. Consumers don't care what they think or say. They care about what they hear, see, believe, trust, experience and then buy. Go forth and build a sustainable brand. The consumer is waiting.

TABLE 5. Key take-aways

What is needed is not a change in consumer behavior but a change in brand behavior
Not all brands are born equal – some are by nature more sustainable than others
Brands fail when they ignore weaknesses and oversell perceived strengths
A sustainable brand is defined by how the product and brand interact and combine

Product sustainability must include both the value chain impact as well as the inherent value of the product itself

Sustainability branding must include both the way a brand connects with the consumer and how it aligns with sustainability

Brands are dynamic and can adapt and change to strengthen their claims as a sustainable brand

The Sustainable Brand Model allows a brand to find its unique sustainable brand value proposition & identify areas of weakness

Reference

Belz, F. and Peattie, K. 2009. *Sustainability Marketing: A Global Perspective* (New York: John Wiley & Sons).

CPSIA information can be obtained
at www.ICGtesting.com
Printed in the USA
LVHW042232230623
750625LV00004B/480